AF884479

Financial Literacy 101 for Teens

It Is Not the Principle It Is the Money

Get Your Piece of The Pie

Carlos A. Gonzales

Copyright © 2026 Carlos A. Gonzales

All Rights Reserved

“
“The most profound investment we can make is in the knowledge of those who will carry our lessons into the future.”
Carlos A. Gonzales

Dedication

I dedicate this book to the McLane High School Business Academy students, the driving force behind Financial Literacy 101 for Teens.

To my family, whose love, support, and encouragement provide daily inspiration to me.

And to the Almighty for His grace and daily blessings.

Acknowledgment

I thank my students at the McLane High School Business Academy for trusting me with their knowledge, thoughts, and financial concerns. I genuinely believe teenagers will benefit from reading this book and following the practical suggestions, solutions, or considerations proposed, regardless of their current financial situation, predicament, or reality.

I also owe credit to all my student bank interns, most notably Melanye Rodriguez Serna, Giyanna Olivas, Melody Moua, and Travis Chang, who have provided insight into the lives of teenagers and shared their thoughts, concerns, and experiences with me, which are at the heart of the instructional lessons and message.

I have been blessed with wonderful teachers, mentors, co-workers, and students, most notably Maria Lepe Preciado, Michael Brionez, Thomas Valentino, Dr. William Rice, Marcie Alejo Gonzales, and Scott Lamm, whose belief and encouragement have inspired my love of learning, natural curiosity, and a desire to help and teach others.

CONTENTS

> "True self-reliance is not the absence of help, but the presence of purpose and the courage to remain a lifelong learner."
>
> — Carlos A. Gonzales

About the Author

Carlos Alberto Gonzales is a lifelong learner and a passionate advocate for financial literacy, community service, self-reliance, and the power of purpose.

With over 20 years of experience in the financial industry, ranging from budget assistant to CEO and over 10 years of experience teaching banking and finance at the high school level, he holds an AA degree in Business Administration from California State Center Community College, Fresno; a Bachelor's degree in Business Administration with an option in Management from California State University, Fresno; a BA degree in Operations, Training, Lending, and Collecting from FORD-Associates First Capital Private University in Dallas, Texas; and a Master's degree in Leadership and Organizational Development from Fresno Pacific University.

In addition, he holds a California Career Technical Education teaching credential in finance and banking, coupled with a California Department of Real Estate (DRE) Broker's License since 2001 (license number 01302224). Carlos and his wife, Marcie, have raised four children and call the California Central Valley home.

"Financial clarity is the shield that protects a young adult from a realm of confusion and the burden of unnecessary debt."
Carlos A. Gonzales
STABILITY

Foreword

Melanye Rodriguez Serna – It is often difficult to find students who know how to manage their finances or even understand what finances refer to. Financial literacy is a vital part of your life that you should embrace. Understanding finances makes life easier. You do not want to leave high school and enter a realm of confusion and lack of knowledge. Many adults today still need to ask for financial advice and even pay for it. So, why pay for every piece of advice when you can read all about it and get ready for life after high school?

Giyanna Olivas – I feel as if every teenager or young adult should read this book. It will help provide knowledge of your finances and how to save and manage your money; it will also help you answer questions in your daily life. This book was written for young adults with the input and experiences of young adults, speaking on our personal financial stories, and we hope these stories help you make better decisions with your money.

Melody Cheeia Moua – You may have grown up around financial literacy your whole life, but it is always important for you to prepare and know how to manage your money into adulthood. You do not want to come out of high school financially unstable, especially with debt. Not only do teenagers struggle with this, but adults also still have issues with financial literacy. This is a great opportunity for you to learn more about financial literacy, manage your money, and avoid unnecessary debt.

Travis Chang – It is surprising that some teenagers today face challenges managing their finances and lack fundamental knowledge about financial literacy. I cannot stress enough the importance of financial literacy and how beneficial it can be in life. You need to understand where your hard-earned money goes and how to manage it properly to achieve financial stability. Take this chance to learn about your money before going into the big world.

This book was written to help introduce Financial Literacy to young people. The goal is to start a conversation that will lead to successful money management and financial freedom.

“Financial Literacy gives you the opportunity to be confident and empowered to live the quality of life you’ve worked for.”
- Erin Beable (Financial Advisor)
HARD WORK
FINANCIAL LITERACY
QUALITY OF LIFE

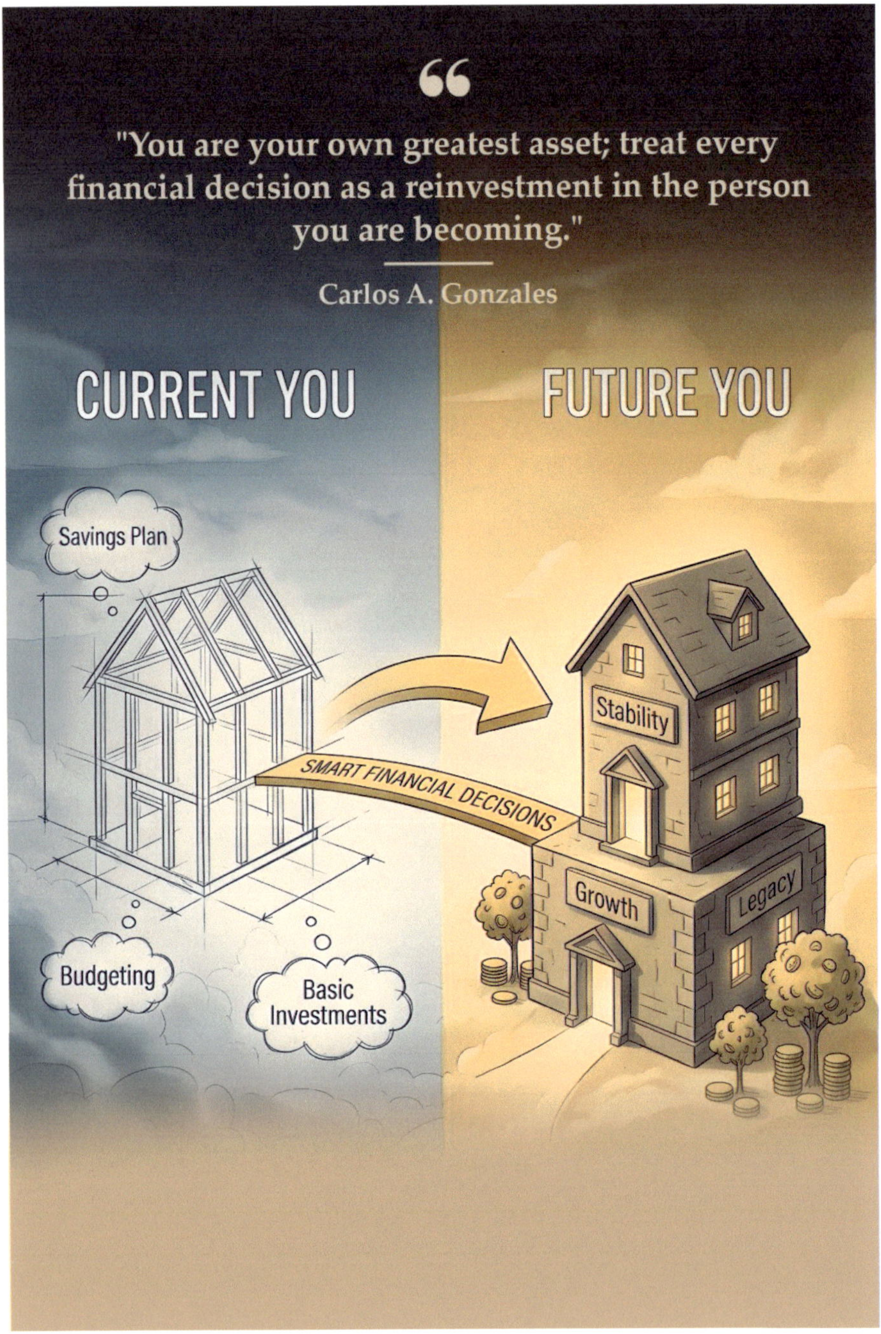
"You are your own greatest asset; treat every financial decision as a reinvestment in the person you are becoming."
Carlos A. Gonzales
CURRENT YOU
FUTURE YOU
Savings Plan
Budgeting
Basic Investments
SMART FINANCIAL DECISIONS
Stability
Growth
Legacy

Preface

My Hope For Young People

Dear young people,

Let me start by telling you something you may already know: life often presents challenges, but you have the power to prepare for them.

Learning about money management is a lifelong skill with different needs, situations, and issues that can separate you from your hard-earned money. I hope that as you read this book, you consider your situation and realize you are an investment.

Many students will graduate high school without an idea of what or who they want to be. However, graduating without financial literacy is a concern and one of the reasons I am in education; the goal is to be part of prevention and not financial rehabilitation.

Feel free to skip around and read different chapters; something will catch your attention, and you will soon find yourself reading this book from cover to cover. As you read, ask yourself, "What lifestyle do I want? What does learning mean to me? What is my experience with money? How can I use the information provided to get a head start on life? What can I do today to improve my tomorrow?"

It is not by chance that you have this book, as everyone will ultimately benefit from understanding financial literacy. Focus on taking financial baby steps and work your way up the financial freedom ladder. You can do it.

Thank you for reading this book and sharing it with others.

All the best.
Carlos Alberto Gonzales

"Financial freedom is not a destination you reach by chance; it is a foundation you build by understanding the tools at your disposal."
Carlos A. Gonzales
FINANCIAL FREEDOM
KNOWLEDGE
DISCIPLINE
STRATEGY
TOOLS

Introduction

As Alan Greenspan, former Chair of the Federal Reserve of the United States, once said, "The number one problem in today's generation and economy is the lack of financial literacy."

It makes sense that the sooner you learn about financial literacy, the more likely you are to thrive financially. Teenagers face the burden of balancing wants and needs against what others can provide and the pressure of must-haves promoted by social media. Long gone are the days of paper routes, mowing yards, odd jobs, and walking around town to collect recycling items. With the minimum wage increasing, teenagers now compete against adults for entry-level positions. Coupled with the inflated cost of living, understanding and applying financial literacy concepts early will provide a foundation for financial freedom.

Financial literacy includes learning about lending and understanding how credit works. The adage that an ounce of prevention is worth a pound of cure is an understatement. Often, teenagers look at finances as a money matter: I have no money, so it does not matter.

As a high school business, finance, and entrepreneurship teacher, students often express fear about paying for school events, college, housing and living expenses, buying a car, managing debt, living paycheck to paycheck, and how to start a business. These fears are real, and for teens, they contribute to the bigger questions: What will I do after high school? What school will I go to? And what do I want to do with my life?

This book will discuss financial literacy concepts, Digital Security, spending habits, high school expenses, credit, setting priorities, and practical ways to take steps towards financial freedom. Specifically, we will introduce and explain the three C's—consciousness, constraint, and creativity to help young people make the best out of what they have, where they are in life, and whatever their financial situation might be.

"Consciousness keeps you present, Constraint keeps you safe, and Creativity turns your limited resources into unlimited opportunities."
Carlos A. Gonzales
OPPORTUNITY
CONSCIOUSNESS
CONSTRAINT
CREATIVITY

Chapter 1 – Financial Literacy Concepts

One of the true blessings in my life was having my great-grandmother around during my childhood. Her message was straightforward and to the point: Just because you can do something does not mean you should. Her words continue to guide and inspire my daily decisions, thoughts, and actions.

Throughout this book, we will talk about, expand, and offer practical ways to incorporate the following three concepts into your daily lives: Consciousness, Constraint, and Creativity.

Teenagers are digital natives. Social media and online influencers are constantly pushing and trying to persuade you to purchase things you do not need. Being conscious or present in the moment will help you understand when people are trying to separate you from your hard-earned money. Show constraint by asking yourself: "Are you able to live without the thing or item being sold?"

The third concept, Creativity, expands and incorporates many parts of your life. As the saying goes, "Necessity is the mother of all inventions." When I was around six years old, my Papa gave me one of the greatest gifts ever. Let me explain: Growing up, money was not a topic of conversation, especially for kids. In our neighborhood, springtime was outside time, and you could see all the kids riding their bikes, skateboards, and roller skating. It was at this time that I would be the recipient of the gift of creativity. My Papa was a very handy person. Since adults never talked about money around kids, I do not know if he did not have the money to buy me a bike, but what I do know is that he did the next best thing: he showed me how to build a bike. After a few trips to the landfill and one awesome Saturday, my first bike—Big Red (yes, the bike was red and had some big tires) was ready. I rode the bike until the tires fell off. I continued to make bikes; they were not always the best-looking bikes, but it was better than walking. To think that a little creativity, coupled with some skill and a lot of desire, created one of the best moments and memories in my life! In a short time, I had eight bikes. Once other kids saw my bike, they wanted my bike, and selling them was a wonderful way to work on my people skills, communication, and make some money.

Think about the things you could make or do to help you live your best life. For example, instead of buying someone a birthday cake, try making a cake or cupcakes. Make them a paper crown and sing "Happy Birthday." Go through your wardrobe and look for ways to make something old new again. Many schools now offer clothing closets, food pantries, and additional resources for students. Think outside the box before spending your money; you might just be giving someone the best gift ever.

Financial literacy is more than learning to manage your money; it is about being independent, self-sustaining, and developing skills and a mindset that will provide new experiences, opportunities, and moments in real time that last a lifetime. Employ the three C's: Consciousness, Constraint, and Creativity in your daily life. Your older self will thank you.

“Your economic security does not lie in your job; it lies in your own power to produce, to think, to learn, to create, to adapt. That is true financial independence; it is not having wealth, it is having the power to produce wealth.”
– Stephen Covey
WEALTH CREATION
THINK
LEARN
CREATE
ADAPT
PRODUCE

Chapter 2 – Banking Basics

Banks, we see them everywhere, in commercials, in stadiums, and at many events. However, when was the last time you talked about what a bank can do for you? Considering the history of banks, especially during the Great Depression of 1929 and the Great Recession of 2008, you might ask yourself why you put your trust, confidence or faith in them.

Understanding what a bank can do is a good start. Realizing that banks will be around as long as there is money and people to use it should provide some comfort. When we think about banking basics, savings, checking, and loans come to mind. As a young person, you are seeing the financial world through the eyes of the adults in your life. Some might have good experiences, and others might have bad experiences. The reality is you are not them and you have an opportunity to learn from them, and understanding what a bank can do for you at a your age is what financial literacy is all about.

To help provide perspective and gather information, 40 high school business students were asked: "How often do you talk about money at home?" Responses: 32.5% said all the time, 60.0% said sometimes, 5% said never, and 2.5% said only when it is bad. Ask yourself: "When do you talk about money, and what are the circumstances or reasons for the conversation?" It has been my experience that people talk about money when they want to buy something, and that is important too. However, focusing on what a bank can do for you and your family is about more than buying stuff; it is about saving, investing, and overall putting plans and goals in place to help you reach your financial freedom objectives. Banks are financial tools; learn to use them.

Banks come in different shapes and sizes. Some are small, called community banks or retail banks. They focus on lending money to certain industries and offering services to small businesses with a few certificates of deposit or savings accounts with limited loan or lending products. Credit Unions are not-for-profit financial cooperatives owned and directed by their members, focusing on personal financial services. Other banks are large and provide services designed for large businesses, such as big transaction accounts, government entities, and institutions; these are called commercial banks. Commercial banks may include investment accounts, business mergers and acquisitions, coupled with access to services worldwide. When we hear the word bank, commercial banks are the ones that come to mind – marketing works.

Banks focus on the three C's: Character, Capacity, and Collateral. Each area is important and vital to your financial freedom. Let us talk about each area for understanding.

Character: What do you think about when you hear the word character? According to Merriam-Webster, character is one of the attributes or features that make up and distinguish an individual. In lending terms, this means what your spending habits are, and in short, do you pay your bills on time?

Capacity: according to Merriam-Webster, capacity is the maximum amount or number that can be contained or accommodated. In lending terms, this refers to your debt-to-income ratio, and in short, do you make or have enough money to pay all your bills or debt?

Collateral: according to Merriam-Webster, collateral is property pledged by a borrower to protect the interest of the lender. In lending terms, do you own physical items of value equal to or greater than the money being borrowed? In short, if you do not repay your loan, what do you have that can be taken as a form of payment?

As a young person, you should be asking yourself how you will acquire Character, Capacity, and Collateral. Although there are many different ways, some practical steps will be presented: First, focus on what you can control. To help support positive Character, open a savings account with your local bank and get to know the branch manager. Once you start working, open a checking account and set up direct deposit; this will help you establish an income history in the event you need a loan. In some cases, you may have an adult in your life with good credit, specifically a credit card. If that person is willing

"Your character is the invisible currency that banks value long before the first dollar is ever deposited or lent."
Carlos A. Gonzales
DEPOSITS
CHARACTER

to add you as an authorized user, the credit reporting bureaus (Trans Union, Equifax, Experian) will report it, and almost overnight, you will have a credit history. In some cases, you may be able to report your positive cell phone account, rent, utilities, and some other accounts you might open with small furniture dealers, electronic stores, or car sales. Once your account has been open for six months, it will provide a positive credit rating, provided that you have paid your bills on time.

Before applying for credit, make sure the business or company reports payment history. Companies pay to have your payment history reported. In many cases, a company will only pay to report payment history with one of the Three Credit Bureaus. Ask and keep track of this information. Keep in mind you are starting your financial history and establishing the foundation of your Character.

Capacity: When you hear the word Capacity, think about debt-to-income. Every lending institution might approve loans a little differently. However, most, if not all, will use your gross income and ask for proof of income (paystubs, tax returns, bank statements, etc.). So on paper, you make or have enough money to qualify, but that does not mean you really have the Capacity to pay the loan back early or on time. Only you know your life and spending habits. Be conscious of that, and remember: Just because you can does not mean you should. Consider your alternatives, and ask yourself: "Is this good debt or bad debt?"

Collateral: You might think you do not have any, but think about it: how much did your shoes, bag, jacket, cell phone, computer, jewelry, and other items cost? They have value, and things or items that have value are Collateral. This is why pawn shops use what you own or have to determine how much they will lend you or pay for your goods. Before you know it, you will own cars, homes, land, artwork, stocks, and other things of value, which will create new opportunities. Ask yourself when buying something: "Does this have value? Will it retain its value over time? Does this add value to my life?" Is this something I can live without?

Several years ago, one of my students was walking down the hall. Imagine someone waddling, lifting their legs and moving them forward, toes pointed outward. The next day, I talked to the student and asked if everything was okay. I saw them walking differently than they regularly do. With a big smile, the response was, "Mr. G, I just bought these new shoes (the fancy ones) and do not want to put creases on them. In about two weeks, I will sell them and make some money (profit), and then I will buy more and keep it going." You see, when spending money, quality and value rarely go out of style. This student had started a business and did not know it, started investing and did not realize it, and started saving money by creating a budget and setting goals without understanding the positive money habits in place. Never discount your age and the things you do today; taking baby steps in the right direction is better than not taking any steps. Imagine you are planting a young tree; in time, with love and care, it will grow and be amazing, just like you.

When I was a young man in high school, I opened my first savings and checking account. I had a small balance; most of my money was spent on life and adulting expenses. At the time, it seemed like the smart thing to do because keeping money on me or in the house was not a good idea. Without knowing it, I started a positive habit of putting money in my savings account each payday. At the time, this bank offered what was called a Christmas club account, like a savings account with limited access (a penalty for taking money out early)—it matured two weeks before Christmas and worked great. This bank product helped me budget when I did not have a budget, imagine that.

I remember the teller sent me to an account manager who helped me understand how to use a checkbook and keep a running balance. They helped me get a credit card and later purchase a new vehicle. Yes, I opened a rainy-day fund account. I called it my "Keep Me On The Road Money" account.

Establishing a relationship with your local bank at a young age is a great way to find out what a bank can do for you. Growing up, I did not have these conversations at home or school. Getting out of your comfort zone is not easy. I remember being nervous, and not knowing what to ask did not help my nerves. Ask yourself: "How do you know what you do not know?" Yes, you can read a book, watch a video, or listen to a podcast, but at the end of the day, your specific questions or needs may not be answered in a way that makes sense to you. More importantly, knowing what you need to do does not mean you will do it. Meeting the account manager and getting one-on-one service was awesome; it helped me open the right account for me, order checks, request a debit card, and gather information in real time. I saved time and money by starting a simple conversation.

Establishing positive relationships and harnessing the courage to get out of your comfort zone to ask questions or for help will set you on a positive course to understanding and managing the money you do have. This will provide confidence, which will inspire you to ask "What is next?" buying your first home, starting a business, or opening a business. Asking your bank what it can do for you will help you make informed financial decisions in the future and help you discover opportunities that will last a lifetime and change not only your life for the better but all those around you. Yes, you can!

“

A small conversation with a financial expert can save you a lifetime of expensive mistakes.

Carlos A. Gonzales

Chapter 3 – High School Expenses

As a high school teacher, I hear from seniors every year that being a senior is expensive; the struggle is real. Take a moment to write down what you consider to be your anticipated senior year expenses. These typically include clothes, shoes, lunch, gas, car maintenance, relationships, entertainment, sports, and clubs, such as Key Club or FBLA. Don't forget the major events: homecoming, sporting events, senior pictures, the yearbook, winter formal, prom, grad night, field trips, and graduation.

Your senior year will go by quickly, almost as fast as your money. To manage this, you must set a budget and stick to it. This requires you to practice consciousness (being in the moment), show constraint (just because you can does not mean you should), and apply creativity to your plans. Start by gathering information and highlighting the events you truly want to experience. Then, put a plan in place using SMART goals (Specific, Measurable, Attainable, Realistic, and Timely). Open a bank account and ask what products the bank offers to help you reach these goals.

One high school expense that often arises is potlucks or classroom events. Some students are not in a position to bring food or drinks, especially if they have multiple classes hosting events at once. In these situations, we discuss the importance of being of value. If you cannot contribute financially, you can still participate by helping with setup, cleanup, organization, or serving. Being of value shows that you care and want to be involved. Your time and effort represent a different form of currency, so always ask the question: "How may I be of service?"

"When your wallet cannot contribute to the cause, let your willingness to serve be your greatest form of currency."

Carlos A. Gonzales

They knew the price included tickets and transportation, but they didn't know if food was allowed on the bus or if the park locker system could be used for snacks to avoid expensive park meals. They also hadn't asked about payment plans, fundraiser opportunities, or final deadlines. Gathering this information makes the decision clearer and reduces stress. Remember, you are only young once; focus on creating positive memories by being informed.

Next, perform a skills inventory to identify potential side hustles. You might qualify for a paid internship, tutor other students, or create websites, designs, and marketing flyers. Perhaps you are skilled at crafts, makeup, or nails. Talk to your school counselor about work permits and let those around you know you are looking for work. Once you begin making money, start saving immediately, pay yourself first, and keep your savings progress private.

Be conscious of spending habits that can spoil your plans, such as food delivery services, video games, or frequent online purchases. Remember: everything is trying to separate you from your money. When considering expenses, be honest about your lifestyle and image. One student realized that between the $380 ticket, a new outfit, shoes, a haircut, and missed wages from work, a single night of fun actually cost $600. Social media has changed the image game, making us feel we need a new fit for every occasion. Before purchasing, ask yourself: "Do I really need this? How many hours must I work to pay for it?"

Be creative, talk to friends or teachers about sponsorships, or look for ways to participate without overspending or wastefulness. Make plans, not excuses.

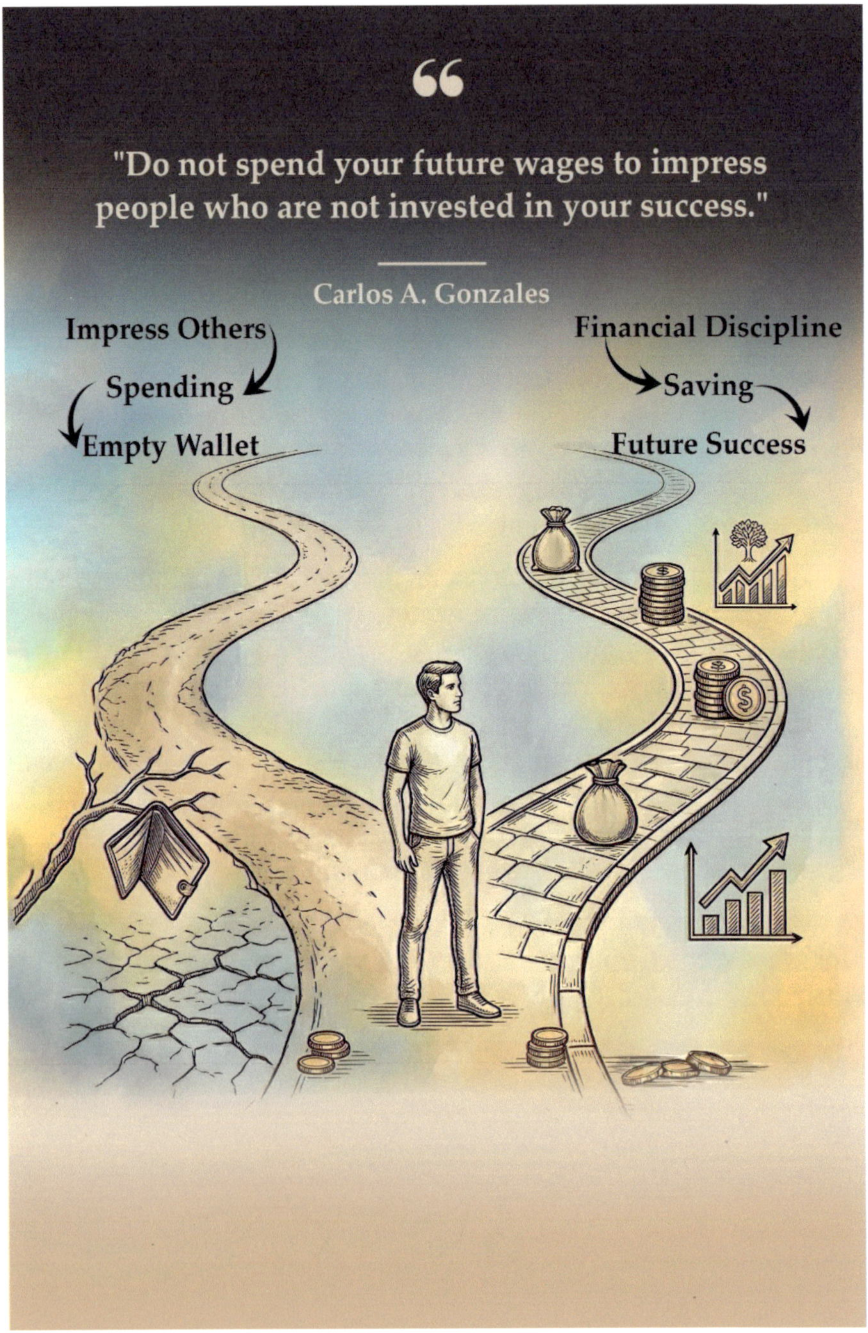
"
"Do not spend your future wages to impress people who are not invested in your success."
Carlos A. Gonzales
Impress Others
Spending
Empty Wallet
Financial Discipline
Saving
Future Success

Chapter 4 – Paying for Education

Every October, the topic of college or continuing education arises in my classroom. As students meet with counselors and start applying to schools, graduation suddenly becomes real. This can be an incredibly stressful time. When people ask the number one senior-year question—"What are you going to do after high school?"—the pressure is immense. Remember: make plans, not excuses. Look for options rather than obstacles, and never lie to yourself about your goals. To help identify your strengths, consider taking free personality or career tests. For instance, the ASVAB test is not just for military recruitment; it is a great tool to provide career options based on your unique skills, abilities, and knowledge.

In business, we use the KISS principle: Keep It Simple, Silly. Find out what low-cost options your school provides to help answer big life questions. Be creative and adventurous by exploring internships (paid or unpaid), volunteer events, and clubs. Remember that knowing what you do not like or are not good at is just as valuable as knowing what you do like and are good at.

What is FAFSA? The Free Application for Federal Student Aid (FAFSA) is your first step toward obtaining money for your education. Many schools host information meetings in November and December to help you get organized. Keep in mind that there are federal and state priority deadlines you must meet to be considered for aid. You must update this application every year, so keep your records in a secure place.

The FAFSA also helps you get pre-approved for student loans if they are necessary. Understanding the difference between subsidized and unsubsidized loans is vital for your financial freedom:

- **Subsidized Loans:** The interest is paid by the government while you are in school.
- **Unsubsidized Loans:** The loan accrues interest immediately, meaning you will eventually owe more than

the original amount borrowed. Consider loans a last resort, but if used wisely, they are an investment in yourself.

Knowing how you will pay for education is as important as knowing why you are pursuing it. Research your career of interest and ask your counselor about Career Technical Education (CTE) Pathways. Don't be afraid to ask for a 15-to-30-minute informational interview with someone in your field. Once you identify a school, calculate the total cost, including tuition, books, housing, transportation, and food. Having a specific number will give your FAFSA application more meaning and purpose.

If you are unsure of your path, consider staying local for the first two years to save money. If you remain undecided, I recommend a degree in business. Understanding the economy and how to manage people applies to every career field.

I grew up in a small town with limited career options. After a car accident sidelined my sports career, my life changed, and my path to college became uncertain. By establishing positive relationships with my mentors, I discovered a job with the Forest Service that led me to the world of budget and finance. Through conversations with my boss, I learned about tuition reimbursement and industry-specific scholarships. I eventually applied for a USDA scholarship that many said was impossible to get, and I won it. Sometimes, all you need to do is dare to try.

Many students fall into the "I know" trap. Life is not easy, and you may face challenges that make finishing school seem impossible. However, people do not plan to fail; they fail to plan. If you stop attending school but have outstanding loans, your bill will arrive after six months, regardless of whether you graduated. Stay in school; take fewer classes if needed, but do not stop.

"Education is an investment in yourself, but the highest returns come to those who dare to try and look for options rather than obstacles."

Carlos A. Gonzales

Beyond traditional grants and loans, explore these avenues:

- **Work-Study:** Campus jobs that help pay for school expenses.
- **Employer Support:** Many companies will pay for your education in exchange for work experience.
- **Public Service Loan Forgiveness (PSLF):** A federal program that may forgive your loans in exchange for working in government, non-profits, or public hospitals.
- **Military Service:** The GI Bill covers tuition, fees, and a monthly living allowance.
- **Science Technology Engineering and Math (STEM):** Targeted toward students pursuing careers in Science, Technology, Engineering, and Mathematics.
- **Hispanic Scholarship Fund (HSF):** Offers scholarships and comprehensive support for students of Hispanic heritage.
- **United Negro College Fund (UNCF):** Provides scholarships and emergency aid specifically for minority students.
- **Community Organizations:** Local clubs, such as Rotary, Kiwanis, Lions, and Shriners, along with state-specific organizations, often provide financial aid or local support.

Be an active participant in your college and career decision-making. Ask yourself: "Besides money, what other forms of support will help me succeed?" Networking with community leaders is an excellent way to gain experience and exposure. Additionally, look for a mentor, someone who is already where you want to be.

As the African Proverb says: "Closed mouths do not get fed." Use consciousness to stay aware of your options, constraint to avoid unnecessary debt, and creativity to find a path that fits your life. You matter, and the decisions you make today will provide value for your future self and family.

Every “no” gets you closer to a “Yes!”

Chapter 5 – Living on Your Own

As a teenager, you might dream about leaving the town, city, or area where you grew up. That is understandable. However, once you start considering your financial situation and adulting responsibilities, thinking realistically about moving out will provide a new perspective. Moving out is a major life event; planning ahead allows you to take the emotion out of the decision and focus on what you actually need to do to make it happen.

Many colleges offer on-campus dorms or off-campus resources to help you make informed housing decisions. However, since advisors do not know your specific lifestyle, you must write down your "must-haves." Consider factors like proximity to public transportation, walking distance to school or work, access to a washer and dryer, and being close to grocery stores, shopping, and entertainment.

To provide perspective, we surveyed forty high school juniors and seniors regarding their plans for living on their own.

Survey Results: Do you have a plan for living on your own?

- **42.50%:** Yes, immediately after high school.
- **30.00%:** Once they start working.
- **27.50%:** Have not yet thought about it.

The reality is that once you graduate, turn 18, or enter the workforce, living on your own becomes a real possibility, whether by choice or life circumstances. Thinking about your living situation now is a vital mental exercise. Will you rent an apartment, a house, a studio, or just a room? If you need roommates, what are the requirements, and how will shared expenses be paid? Have you considered the cost of renters insurance, parking, internet, electricity, and cooking supplies?

As you start adulting, make a list of priorities: distinguish your needs from your wants. Establish a monthly budget and break it down into specific pay periods. For example, if your monthly food budget

"Independence is the freedom to choose your responsibilities before your circumstances choose them for you."

Carlos A. Gonzales

is $400, and you get paid twice a month, allocate $200 from each paycheck to cover your meals.

When considering large purchases like furniture, a TV, a computer, or a car, be realistic and ask yourself: "Do I really need this right now?" Also, consider the logistics of your move. If you sign a one-year lease, who will move your belongings? Will you need a truck? How easy is it to move large items into your new place? Apply the concept of constraint here: just because you can purchase something does not mean you should.

Living on your own can be scary, so it is important to find ways to keep yourself motivated and focused. I was once inspired by a student who shared how they stayed driven. They told me that their family would drive through nice neighborhoods to imagine their future there. This student used those moments to plan a path that included education, a professional career, and a business.

By beginning with the end in mind, this student became a student banker, started a business, and was willing to make sacrifices to fit their long-term plan. I have no doubt that someday, people will be driving through the neighborhood that the student calls home.

Focus on the things you can control. Use consciousness to stay present in your financial decisions, show constraint with your spending, and use creativity to make the most of your current resources. Ask questions, do your best to avoid spending money you do not have, and remember that your current living situation is often temporary. Keep it that way as you build toward your future and financial freedom.

What drives you today will sustain you tomorrow, provided you have the courage to expand your comfort zone and accept the challenge life has to offer.

"Building generational wealth does not start with a large paycheck; it starts with a mindset that values keeping money over merely making it."

Carlos A. Gonzales

Chapter 6 – Building for Tomorrow

As a career technical education teacher, I tell all my students: You are an investment. As you start to build for tomorrow, remember that your number one investment should be yourself.

When students talk to me about life, they often want to know about investing, college, or starting a business. I tell them it is not just about making money; it is about keeping the money you make. As you plan your future, taking baby steps is essential. Often, when people focus solely on making money, they lose sight of the people and values around them. This can lead to taking two steps backward for every step forward.

Building for tomorrow requires living in the present while considering the generations that will come after you. I am a first-generation US citizen, and realizing the struggles my grandmother endured to bring our family here is humbling. Whether you are the first in your family to go to university, buy a house, or build a business, you must plan for tomorrow while enjoying the present.

Teenagers today face unique concerns: getting stuck in jobs they dislike, falling into debt, and managing their mental wellness. Social media heavily influences your decisions, but you must remember that true generational wealth starts with your mindset, habits, and behaviors. Children and peers learn more from what you do than what you say. By developing better spending habits now, you influence your entire family circle.

In our digital age, it is easy to take security for granted. Digital security is a vital part of protecting your future. When selecting a financial partner, use consciousness to ask the following questions:

- What is the bank's financial footprint?
- What security measures protect my information?
- Is there a clear process to help me if my account is hacked?
- Is there a department dedicated to helping me rebuild my credit or recover funds?

Many students fear debt. Before making a purchase, ask yourself: "How many hours will I have to work to pay this off?" Remember, a minimum payment is designed to keep your credit in good standing, not to pay off your debt quickly. Before taking a loan, verify the interest rates, terms, and any pre-payment penalties.

If you find yourself in debt, use these practical steps to pay it off:

- **List all debts:** Include balances, interest rates, fees, and due dates.
- **Prioritize:** Focus on the debt with the largest balance and highest interest rate.
- **Pay Strategically:** Make the minimum payment on other loans, but make a larger-than-normal payment on the high-interest loan.

Saving money is just as valuable as making it. Imagine you are planting a tree that will grow over time. Consider these strategies to help your money grow:

- **Low-Risk Options**: Interest-bearing savings accounts, Certificates of Deposit (CDs), or mutual funds.
- **Stocks:** Invest in companies that share your values or produce products you already use. This helps you stay motivated to research your investments.
- **Diversification:** Avoid putting all your money in one place; spread your investments to manage risk.

The Three C's in Action: To build a successful future, employ the core concepts of this book:

- **Consciousness:** Be in the moment with your spending. Avoid passive spending where you lose track of where your money goes.
- **Constraint:** Just because you can afford it does not mean you should buy it. Avoid spending money to impress people.
- **Creativity:** If you cannot afford an expensive gift, be of value. Volunteer to help set up, clean up, or organize an event. Your time and effort are a form of currency that people will remember.

As an accounting friend once told me: "You cannot write off what you do not write in." Be present in the moment. You should never be so broke that you are not able to pay attention.

Building for tomorrow starts today, and it begins with you. What is right for you and your family may not be the right path for others, and that is perfectly fine. The key is to start building little by little; this steady, incremental progress helps you avoid paralysis by analysis. We all know people who talk about their plans but never take action, those who have the dream but lack the drive, and those who find excuses instead of solutions.

Ask yourself: What are the things that matter most? What do you want to build? Who do you want to be? Only you can define your success, and only you have the power to turn your goals and dreams into a reality.

When I started college, life was not easy. Adulting and life's circumstances presented a reality I was not prepared for; with my faith in hand and gumption in my steps, building for tomorrow was my primary focus. Every day, my mindset was: "Yes, I can." With confidence in the Almighty and the power of purpose and positive thinking, your future is brighter than you can imagine. Yes, you can!

"A budget is not a restriction on your freedom; it is a plan for your peace of mind."

Carlos A. Gonzales

Chapter 7 – The Effects Finances Have on Mental Health

A penny for your thoughts. During my time in consumer finance, I often met with people who were struggling to pay their bills. Once we began putting a plan in place, it frequently opened the door to a deeper conversation. They spoke about being unable to sleep, being scared to answer the phone, and, in many cases, facing the breakup of relationships and a general difficulty focusing. Today, we recognize this as a mental health concern. It pays to understand that your financial health is directly linked to your mental wellness.

If you are reading this, financial literacy has likely touched your life in some way. After many conversations with teenagers, it is clear that financial struggles do not just affect one person; they impact everyone around them. I have seen students take on adulting responsibilities to help their parents, sometimes missing school to work extra hours, babysit, or take on a second job to keep the family afloat or put food on the table.

At times, having a budget or saving money might feel like a punishment or a wasted effort. In reality, it is an investment in your mental health. Emergencies happen to everyone; the question is: Will you be prepared? Establishing good spending habits helps you take control of your money. A budget is not a punishment; it is a plan that allows you to tell your money where to go instead of wondering where it went. Money can feel like a leaking faucet that never stops: make plans, not excuses.

One conversation stands out: a student who was a valedictorian candidate, a student-athlete, and active in school events, suddenly changed. They went from having 100% attendance to less than 70% and became very reserved. Because we had a good relationship, we sat down to talk. With a straight face and teary eyes, the student shared that the adults in their home had their car impounded due to a lack of valid registration and insurance. This led to an inability to pay for rent or food. With younger siblings at home, living on the streets was not an option. The student had been missing school for weeks to work and help pay the bills. The stress was visible, and the struggle was real.

Right now, you are living the life the adults around you have created. Soon, you will be making your own decisions and living with the consequences, both positive and negative. Financial literacy is a key tool to help reduce mental stress, allowing you to be fit in mind, body, and spirit. To achieve this, focus on the three C's: Consciousness, Constraint, and Creativity when navigating your wants and needs.

It is not easy to say "no" to things that seem fun or exciting. However, your mental health is your responsibility. Sometimes, saying no to others is the best way to say "yes" to yourself. Learning to live within your means creates positive habits that will eventually allow you to say yes to opportunities you never imagined. Remember: people do not plan to fail; they fail to plan. You are an investment. Do not take yourself too seriously, but take what you do seriously.

I had a professor who once said, "Pressure is what others place on you; stress is what you place on yourself." Take some time to think about the unnecessary pressures affecting your mental health and work toward minimizing them. Baby steps are better than no steps. Start today to take control of your life and your health. Time goes by faster than you think. How would you like to spend it? Keep in mind that there is only one you, and you are worth the investment.

During my time in consumer finance, there was a common saying: “Once a consumer finance customer, always a consumer finance customer.” I have always disliked this outlook. Instead, I have dedicated my time, energy, and resources to helping others realize they have the power to take control of their finances. By doing so, you can relieve a major cause of mental stress.

Start by talking about finances with others and asking yourself: "What can a bank do for me?" and "What am I willing to do right now, today, to change my circumstances?" Remember, there are people and resources available to help you; it simply takes the courage to get out of your comfort zone and ask for help, support or advise.

Keep in mind, life happens, just because you have a plan does not mean they won't or can't change, focus on the things you can control or make decisions on, realize and accept everything that happens is for a reason. Life and other people will try to upset, frustrate, or challenge your peace of mind; it is during this moment that you should take a deep breath and realize that you are in control of your mental health, and you are stronger than you think. By applying consciousness to your life choices, constraint to your spending habits, and creativity to help you manage the wants in life and your financial goals, you can build a future that supports your financial, social, and mental well-being goals, objectives, or dreams.

Think positively even when things go wrong, stay focused when life gets crazy, and continue to move forward even when you don't think you can.

Every day presents a new challenge; embrace it!

Epilogue

Learning to work with people and manage money are two skills that will never go out of style. Finance is a pillar of society and should be a topic of conversation. I hope you will start a conversation today.

Financial literacy is more than a set of rules; it is a lifelong process and a daily endeavor. As you prepare for the next chapter in your life, think about the things and people that matter to you, think about the lifestyle you want to live, and focus on what it will take to make it happen. Remember, the goal is not to get things, it is to keep the things and people in your life that matter the most.

As you move forward, remember to remain conscious in your decision-making, exercise constraint when managing your money and relationships, and use your creativity to build the best life possible.

I truly wish you all the best.

"Financial literacy is a lifelong marathon of small, conscious decisions. Keep walking, keep learning, and keep growing."
Carlos A. Gonzales
INVEST
GROW
LEARN
SAVE
INVEST

Made in the USA
Monee, IL
05 November 2026

67378082R00029